MW01233425

BETTER THAN

OXY

E. Gomer Meadows

ISBN 978-1-63885-233-9 (Paperback)
ISBN 978-1-63885-249-0 (Hardcover)
ISBN 978-1-63885-234-6 (Digital)

Covenant Books, Inc.
11661 Hwy 707
Murrells Inlet, SC 29576
www.covenantbooks.com

Gomer was a name once spoken upon me, just as there has likely been many names, labels spoken upon you. Names, labels, curses (especially those laced with a few scriptures of the self-righteous) are pebbles thrown by the truly afflicted. There just happens to be no shortage of pain, evil, and affliction in this world. So pebbles can carry the damage of boulders, and (if friendly fire) one or two pebbles can feel like an unending rain of hail. Raise your shield and remember they are mere pebbles! Use them (the names and labels) to heal and free others that lay in the wake of the afflicted. Use them to compel you to see God's promises through. Then from the peaks of Kilimanjaro, toss them away!

CONTENTS

PROLOGUE

An Invitation to You

This collection of poetry (and prose) presents the struggle of everyday disappointments, pain, and challenges in both an in-the-moment and retrospective light. By doing so, it juxtaposes the valleys of our natural mind or perspective with the peaks of our spiritual/renewed perspective. This is done with the hope that you recognize the plot of the enemy (in the valley) versus the promise of God.

Recognition of voices, thoughts, and whelms that aren't of God is of grave importance. It is life or death, literally. The Biblical scripture Romans 12:2 speaks of the process of mind renewal:

> Do not conform to the pattern of this world, but be transformed by the renewing of your mind. Then you will be able to test and approve what God's will is—His good, pleasing, and perfect will.

We do not always appreciate the renewal process as it is gradual and not very satisfying. We may not even fully understand that the primary agent at work in that process is the Word. So the poetry and prose (written from the peaks) on the pages that follow will include scripture references that can be found in the Word of God. This is the only voice strong enough to silence that of suicide, self-hate, and insecurity. His is the only voice true enough to identify the traps others lay for us and deliver us from the snares our brokenness would devise for ourselves.

Mind renewal takes time (a lifetime!), but life waits for no one. That means the challenges will keep rolling no matter where we are in the process. We also know this world offers lots of escapes! Some may work for a spell but will eventually land us right back here to reckon with the pain. So I learned to trust Him (above me) until my perspective and coping mechanisms became more influenced by His Word! This collection speaks to that lesson in trust as well as the day-by-day renewal process that is *better than oxy*.

In your most challenging hours (your valleys), find your anguish in these pages and then stand with me on the peaks of God's wisdom, love, and promises.

ON EMOTIONAL ABUSE

Natural Perspective

For decades, I was content with laughter.
It meant I was heard,
even if I were the butt of the joke.
Some value is better than none.
Plus I seemed to have
an abundance of material,
like things I should have known but didn't.
So I stood in line
like a grateful indigent
and waited for molded bread, saying
"I can always scrape the mold off.
They wouldn't have fed me something inedible.
And who am I to turn my nose up!
I've survived thus far off worse."

For years, I totted an empty bag.
I thought it promising
but far too worn to be coveted.
And I am to blame.
I kept reaching into my heart's chambers
grabbing Lilies and Dandelions
to lay them all
among your treasures

in exchange for something…anything
even if it were broken and unfixable
or carried the stench of the dumpster
where you retrieved it…
I would have had a bag worth tooting
And I wouldn't be in this line.

Spiritual Perspective

Since when did
"Fearfully and wonderfully made"
require a human's gauging

Their opinions, their standards,
and approval
when *I* did *all* the creating

Since when did
"Plans to prosper and not harm you"
require a human's confirming

Their club, class systems,
and terms
when *all* belongs to *Me*

Since when did
the temple I inhabit fall subject to
the puppetry of their conceit

For both our sakes
pick up your armor
recognize the enemy

*"For I know the plans I have for you," declares the Lord, "plans
to prosper you and not to harm you, plans to give you hope
and a future against spiritual wickedness in high places."*
—Jeremiah 29:11

*I praise you because I am fearfully and wonderfully
made; your works are wonderful.*
—Psalms 139:14

ON OLD WOUNDS

Natural Perspective

So you want to talk?
You're young, just stand there by the door.

And distance yourself from the walls.
Don't want them stained by your body oil.

No, for God's sake, not on the bed
If you must, sit here, on the floor.

I sent a box at Christmas.
Don't know how we forgot yours.

No, I wouldn't say pretty
but you have some *okay* features.

Me? I used to walk across campus
and they'd be calling from the bleachers.

You can trust me:
proven counselor, minister, teacher.

You can even talk to a girl I've counseled.
She'll tell you I'm a secret keeper.

When you get in from work tonight,
my hair needs a press.

When you finish cleaning, do not tarry.
Hurry and get dressed.

You will be of use this eve,
waiting on our guests.

Yes, this means something.
My Love Language is Acts of Service. [1]

When you finish sweeping,
come, at once, to my lair.

Just then, when you held that dustpan,
who were you bending over for, dear?

While bent in your Act of Service,[2]
you exposed the top of your underwear.

You seductress spirit,
How long must you be here!

This is why I told them all
about your sordid past.

The childhood abuse, how lost you are,
they all understand, at last!

You don't belong and never will
you nor your miserable clan.

This is why I told them all
the many ways you're less than.

---

[1] *Five Love Languages* book by Gary Chapman.
[2] Ibid.

Spiritual Perspective

How long will you be captive
to the remembrance of
those who act in "honor of Me."
Does that look and feel like Love?

Those wounds will drive you
to chasms dark and damp,
to pick up your poison
and lay down your lamp.

As the ocean receives deposits
from rivers and streams;
those wounds transfer self-hate
to every organ and extremity.

If I had stopped at captive,
stopped at chasms or the wounds
What good would I be to the world
What good, My child, to you?

You cannot stop at evil
stop at malice or envy
I see what you cannot
I see "greater works than these."

Very truly I tell you, whoever believes in me will do the
works I have been doing, and they will do even greater
things than these, because I am going to the Father.
                                          —John 14:12

ON SUBSTANCE ABUSE

Natural Perspective

i am contained
familiar to none
in a crowd that spans lands
oceans and ghosts of the gone

i am nameless
caged but free
breathing but unborn
unheard but screaming

my veins carry death
my way unmarked
my chorus is this
turn your eyes, dear God

Spiritual Perspective

Addiction knows me well
He mocks me openly
Laughing wildly as it would appear
I claw to gain each inch.

My mind wanders to where I left You
Emptied the vial and yanked away
I ran for the darkest hole I could find
Intoxicated with shame

My choices had yielded a doom
From which there was no escape
In a murky gutter, I waited
The vultures, they never came.

I cried myself to sleep
And there covering me were
Three pillars reaching into the night
With winged warriors posted at each

I knew Mercy in that moment
The way I first did a lifetime ago
Since then, in the hours most dire
I look for the Pillars as opposed to the Hole

For he will conceal me there when troubles
come; he will hide me in his sanctuary.
—Psalm 27:5

ON GIVING UP

My senses returned to me. I was exhausted, wheezing for relief, and unaware of the details that led to my current whereabouts. I stretched atop a small bed, stiffened every possible muscle, and then relaxed. For the next few hours, I peered into the light filament—in hopes to remember—reading underneath a willow, sheltering at a quiet abandoned village, or washing in the rain. These were my escapes. It is called disassociation, and it had become involuntary. It was as if my brain had learned from an early age to create a haven for my spirit to run to during the horrid moons, when my body was not able.

I had not longed for them for some time—the willow, the village, the rain—but now I was heavy and unmovable, like an old oak or cedar. The moment weakened my stomach. Until finally I was bent in a fetal position, in prayer that I be lifted never to see this world again.

I searched myself. My limbs were chainless and free. My walls were close, white, and cushioned like a pillow. My body was weak. My heart pounded almost audibly. I had nothing except time, a very low bed, and—gradually—my remembrance. Suddenly solitude was not comforting anymore. Like an avalanche, random images threatened to overtake me. The darkness. The sirens. The stretcher. The questions. The uniforms. The night. The stares. The feeling that my demons had finally caught up to me.

My cell door opened, and a woman appeared.

"A visitor came by and wanted to know how you were doing. How *are* you doing?"

"I want to go home."

"We can't grant that. I'm sorry."

I opened myself, climbed within, and shut the door. I searched the clutter—the ruins. I searched for a song but found nothing. There was no scripture, no melody, no trumpet, no living thing, no willow, no village, and no sanctuary. There was nothing. My shout echoed in the hollow tomb.

The closet. The darkness. The cold floor. The knocking. The vigorously rattling knob. The hysteric pleading, "Open the door. Open the door." The sirens. The questions. The cool night air.

My breath escaped me in the flashing of it all. I didn't hear her question—the lady standing in the doorway.

"So are you okay? How do you feel?"

"I want to go home. I won't survive here."

"Here in the hospital or here in Georgia? What do you mean you won't survive?"

"Will you let me go? Please!"

"When someone tries to take their own life, they are a threat to themselves. We simply cannot release you in this condition."

"What! I was only trying to get to sleep. I couldn't sleep. I was trying to get to sleep!"

"I'm sorry. This is the best we can do right now."

The door shut with a "—and that's final."

She was gone, but her words remained—"take their own life," "in this condition," "they are a threat." Then revisited the darkness. The closet. The rattling knob. The uniforms. The questions. "Are there any other bottles? Are there any others?" I watched the men as they searched for answers. "Do you know if she has any more? Do you know if she has any more?"

I remembered the hours before the closet and pills. There was a walk. I remembered the cool night air. The phone call and the letter stating that there was yet another hearing. Another need to turn around and go back. Another need to speak of that which I had survived—that which I wanted to suppress. I could hear my chains dragging the pavement. I remembered the shaking.

The prayer—

"God, we sing that 'you never put more on us than we can bear.' I cannot find it written. I don't know that it's true, but I'm at my end

12

here. I can't feel you. If you're with me, show me. Show me like you showed Gideon or Joshua. Show me that I'm not fighting alone, like you showed Elisha. Please!"

Now the wait. The hours desperate for sign. The feeling of wanting to sing but only being capable of sobbing the words.

I feel like going on,
I feel like going on.
Though trials come on every hand,
I feel like—

I remembered the hike and the night air. The closet. The bottles. The solitude. The rattling knob. The cold floor. The darkness. Now the padded walls.

I rose from the bed in the white room. I became restless at the thought of confinement. Uneasy at the notion of another label or *condition* attached on account of *having been through something so horrible*. I felt depleted, but the real detriment was that I believed that I was. It was all there now—my recollection of how I had gotten here. I laid all of me atop the bed, piece by piece, with the care like that which might be given to a corpse when laid in a casket.

I lay still and the images came like vultures but with voices from the past—clear and familiar. They brought with them every parasite and every beast to which I thought I had succumbed. I surveyed my spirit. It was broken, bleeding. I knew these beasts that were coming, and they loved blood. So I laid atop the bed in my white room and washed in the rain, then lost myself in the abandoned village awaiting the break of day.

Reflection

The passage speaks of the term *disassociation*. *Disassociation* is "the process of disconnecting or separating from something." I can share from experience that sometimes we disassociate (or disconnect) from people or events in our lives when there is pain associated with them. This is especially so when those painful situations are beyond our control. The danger of disassociation (and most other forms of escape) is the false sense of security it yields. Yes, it is an escape. It is a temporary one. Unfortunately, one of life's unescapable lessons is that a problem unresolved is a problem worsened.

1. Are there situations/circumstances that you are escaping today?
2. If so, what are they (people, life events, recurring circumstances)? Stand toe to toe with it here and now.
3. The most important part of coming out victoriously is getting through it. If we give up (escape, run, stop) while getting through, there is only one sure end. I can assure you *that* end will fall quite short of all that it could be. God promises us that He has plans "to give you hope and a future" (Jeremiah 29:11). Write down the vision, the plan, the dream that is yours. Note: If you do not know Him personally, He is the *only one* I have known to consistently love past words—the *only one* who will not lie. He keeps it 100, Monday through Sunday. What He says in Jeremiah 29:11 is real.
4. While what you wrote for Reflection question number two may not mirror what is listed for Reflection question number three, the same *planner* that Jeremiah 29:11 talks about is in control of it all. He is the one who will transition you from number two to number three. Can you trust that?

ON PERSEVERANCE

Natural Perspective

After the singing
the sweating, the tears
the convulsions that would
on any other grounds
warrant hospitalization

The jumping over pews
and over the slain
laying lifeless as possums or
twitching like addicts

After the oil dousing
the hollering like Mama died
the running, the dancing
and the benediction

I returned unable to recall
message or hymn
wondering if I—too—could twitch
would I then want to live?

Spiritual Perspective

From pew to parking lot
From lot to scorched leather
Kissed by relentless August rays
Thighs singed to the seat
The heat, a reminder of
The everyday hell that awaits

The drive from lot to home
Was loud and blue
Manacles rattling against the brakes
The steeple kept shrinking
In the rearview—until
Finally—it shrunk away

Eyes now ahead, there it was
Holding for dear life
On the window shield
An unsightly yet spirited bug
Windbeaten and barely
Grasping by just one limb

Hanging through bump and jostle
Speed curve and turn
Seeing the spattered guts of prior hims
Clinging though all was
Beyond his control—clinging
In bold refusal to yield

Ah—I know just the thing
Fondling windshield wash controls
Here's to a little unexpected shower
The water pushed him to the edge
Just beyond the wiper's reach
He repositioned with superbug power

I pulled over
Though shook, he took flight
I resolved right there and then
With or without steeple
Love, friend, or hymn
I'll not be outdone by a bug again

> *Not only so, but we also glory in our sufferings, because we*
> *know that suffering produces perseverance; perseverance,*
> *character; and character, hope. And hope does not put us*
> *to shame, because God's love has been poured out into our*
> *hearts through the Holy Spirit, who has been given to us.*
> —Romans 5:3–5

ON DISCERNING WOLVES AND PURPOSE

Natural Perspective

Information is what they hunted.
Behind the weekend pedis,
prayer calls and feel-good moments
something was lurking.
The months of traded stories,
fasting for an answer
and interpreting dreams
it all had a purpose.

Advantage is what they sought.
My "haves" and "wish I hads,'"
my tried and fails,
the "whens" and juicy "hows."
For their fellowship and guidance
I followed and exposed my wounds
now multiplied, gapping open
and ever spilling now.

Spiritual Perspective

There are those who
orgasmically thrive in the
misdirection of others
They quietly release
a long-held sigh
because they are not alone

There are those who
squeeze every detail
every drip of squalor and torment
Tilting their necks back
with tongues erect to feed
that which grows within them

There are those who
will call you among the ruins
saying here is where you are safe
In your shadow, they'll dust
your tracks from the sand
guiding you sweetly into the dark distance

Do not look to others
for the answers
only I can give
You are as I was—
a foreigner with a purpose
only I can reveal

*I will instruct you and teach you in the way you should go; I will
counsel you with my loving eye on you. Do not be like the horse or the
mule, which have no understanding but must be controlled by bit and
bridle or they will not come to you. Many are the woes of the wicked,
but the Lord's unfailing love surrounds the one who trusts in him.*
—Psalms 32:8–10

ON SELF-PERCEPTION

Her sense of self was not erected overnight, over weeks, or over months. Construction commenced as early as elementary school and continued throughout adolescence and into her teens. It was then, in elementary school, that she was first confronted with the misery of insufficiency. Humiliation—like waiting to be picked by one of two captains to play on a team during recess. Waiting and waiting and waiting until inevitably she was the last to be picked—at which point there was no decision to be made at all. Then hearing some peers, esteemed at a standard beyond reach, begrudgingly mumble, "I guess I'll have to take her." Insufficiency—like realizing that a cousin or friend enjoyed her company at home after school but *definitely* not during or on the way to and from. Of all that was within me, it was *she* (the one with the childlike longing) that I feared the most.

So one day, she inquired as to what it was about her that was so undesirable. She was eager to correct the issue at all costs, no matter what it was. Her heart listened as if it dared miss its opportunity to be redeemed and burden free. And so it was revealed—the undesirable—her innocence. Not that she wasn't the exact same age as her peers but that she looked like it. And *that* was unacceptable.

"Look at your chest. You look like an ironing board. And your clothes are always too big. Look at the way you dress."

"Well, what can I do to fix it? Will you help me?"

"Well, I ain't Jesus. But I'll see what I can do."

As promised, her counsel began. The first order of business—"Every other day, take an egg, crack it, and rub it on your chest." She was to keep rubbing regularly until the lumps got bigger and comparable to every other girl in her class. The rubbing would stimulate growth in the glands. And if one morning, she didn't have an egg, she was instructed to use petroleum jelly. Secondly she would be given a bag of clothes after school that day. The drop would take place in the park across the street from her home. She was to start immediately wearing them. They were more stylish and sexier. In addition, she was to stop wearing plats and bangs. Nobody wore those anymore. And burn the bows! Her survival was only ensured the sooner she realized she could not be a little girl anymore.

From deep within, swelled spite for her youth and all it represented. Soon every piece of fabric either got tighter, shorter, thinner, or all of the above—able to be tucked away underneath a plaid button-down and pair of loose-fitting jeans. That is, at least until she could slip into the nearest nook on or close to school property and properly prepare for the day. There in that nook, be it a school bathroom stall or an abandoned shed in proximity to the bus stop, she would paint her innocence with desperation.

The seed was rejection. The harvest was isolation and low esteem. Low like the destination of a child with a cement block chained to her ankle just before she is dropped into an abyss. So low that love of any kind, even that which smelt, tasted, looked, and felt like decaying flesh, was graciously embraced and even actively protected. Of all within me, it was *she* (the one with the childlike trust) who I feared the most.

Ironically her king *slipped one foot in with a "No."*

"Do you have any idea how pretty you are?"

"No."

"None of the boys at school have ever told you that you're pretty?"

"No."

"Well, you are to me."

In the beginning, she was convinced that this was a classic case of pity or charity, but both pity and charity were sufficient to replenish her tank.

"You know—you got *quite a set on you.*"

She immediately glanced down at her chest and thought to herself, *My goodness, the eggs must have worked.*

"Eyes, I mean. Your eyes! They are intriguing."

"Oh—what's that mean?"

"It means that your eyes make people want to know things."

"Things like what?"

"Things like what's behind those eyes—in your head? What are you thinking? What makes you smile, laugh? What do you want?"

Silence fell between them as she pondered the questions awhile. Silence and stillness, but he never got bored. He waited with patience, confidence, and purpose.

"Well, I was thinking I like your rings. Did they cost a lot?"

"Yes, they did. So if I were to give you one, what would you give me?"

He was familiar and, therefore, already welcomed beyond her barriers. More critically, there was a sinkhole within her, for which he convincingly presented a solution. Intrigue was within reach. Intrigue was achievable, like riding a bicycle for the very first time—scared but assured that a strong hand was on the seat. Increasing speed, uphill and down, with comfort and confidence. Then glancing back. Oh, what security ignorance can foster. The solitude. The achievable.

She retreated into her custom-made reality where everything undesirable or dangerous was made acceptable and friendly. The rain. The darkness. The violence. The pedophile. She lay among it all, pacified by the achievement of what she had suffered long to find—approval. It was her senses that first deteriorated. It was *she* (the one who sought to please) whom I had grown to fear the most. She who dug up a laugh when fear and pain flooded her temple. She who prized the contentment of all before reflecting once on her own. She who had rather been selected a host of the vile than be the unchosen.

Reflection

1. Think back to when you first put down your lens of inno-
    cence and began to view your world (and you) differently.
    What events shaped your perception? Were they pleasant?
    Were they welcomed?
2. Sometimes those initial experiences remain active contrib-
    utors to our current self-perception and life choices, far
    longer than we realize. They act as back-end scripts that
    inform our actions and reactions. In what ways have the
    experiences in Reflection question number one informed
    who you are today?

ON PARENTING

Natural Perspective

Before they were
Misguided
enamored by those who lyrically glorify
booty and Benjamins

Before they were
Thirsty
on knees and palms in urine stained
stalls of schools and gas stations

Before they were
Pronounced
for lack of drive, soul
Or brain activity—

They were
Cinderellas
with gowns, castles, and dreams
consistent with their name—Royalty

Spiritual Perspective

That which we do not understand
actions they dare try to justify
to include every pattern existing
even those unrealized

like deceitfulness which precedes
the sting of indifference
or the manipulation that follows
bouts of utter selfishness

all that we abhor
and all that we discern
the sacrifices for which
gratitude would be an ample return

the heartache, the disappointment
purge and gather it all collectively
now throw "as far as the east is from the west"
do this each day respectively

Then, our Father can equip us
to nurture beyond our nature
and our tongues can awaken in them
the life-giving love of our Savior

For the way we forgive
mirrors the way we train
our imitation of the character of Christ today
stops tomorrow's progression of decay

What you have learned and received and heard and seen in me—
practice these things, and the God of peace will be with you.
—Philippians 4:9

As far as the east is from the west, so far has he
removed our transgressions from us.
—Psalms 103:12

ON COMPROMISE
(IN RELATIONSHIPS)

Natural Perspective

I opened myself
And without fear
All within me emptied
As if it were foretold
That he would say, "Yes"
To what was ours to seize

I held him
With all I had
As if I carried his name
Believing his tracks on my body
Would bear purpose
The minute he felt the same

I closed my eyes
Dove from the cliffs
And stretched atop the Atlantic
Our flesh was fluid
With a rhythm of tides
This time will surely yield commitment

I found rest those nights
And dreamt deeply
Of a love that he said was my own
As long as we were the tides
I stayed near shore and
Continued to drift home

Spiritual Perspective

I waited for you
where you vowed you'd be
the very hour
the very day

No other in your life
would remain so faithful
should years go unanswered
still, I wait

I searched your words
thinking maybe
you would acknowledge
you forgot

Or simply miss me
and the sound of my voice
turnabout to seek
our quiet spot

I keep finding myself
watching you while you sleep
your tendency to
cup your head in your hand

I keep replaying
all I desire to say
should you give me
a moment's chance

*Neither height nor depth nor anything else in all creation will be able
to separate us from the love of God that is in Christ Jesus our Lord.*
—Romans 8:39

ON CHARM AND
BEAUTY

Natural Perspective

Bristle removal moments
Now more frequent
By the week

'cause baby cheeks
on spruce limbs
ain't exactly *pink*

from razor-clean crops
to thread-suspended locks
even while he sleeps

from na-tu-ral
to concealer perfect
ver-sa-tile is *pink*

the jiggle, gyrate pro combo
with a hint of
"It's all so new to me."

The compromises that
make-him-remember
everything between is *pink*

Spiritual Perspective

Should the meadow be filled
from edge to edge
with oils and savors
spellbinding as potions
flowers of all nations
and of the rarest sorts
every petal firm and supple
flawless and open

You'd need not call for Me
to make yourself noticed
jumping among the rest
pleading and shouting
you'd need not change
either your scent or essence
to ensure that you are picked
and not forgotten.

For this is the field
of My choosing
the hours we share
are the only hours
the song you sing to Me
is the only chorus
and in this field—
You are the *only* flower

> *Charm is deceptive, and beauty is fleeting; but a*
> *woman who fears the Lord is to be praised.*
> —Proverbs 31:30

ON CODEPENDENCY

Natural Perspective

search for me
when you perish with fatigue
panting as if it were written
your relief is my burden

need me
for you are only noticed
when shadowed by
shoulders broader than your own

stand with me
void to void
knowing inevitably
i will always tower you

revere me
i am your senses
your balance, your best days
and your release

Spiritual Perspective

i had missed too many breezes
reading underneath the willow
or running hand in hand with faith
in overgrown pastures.

i couldn't remember the last time
that I created something
or imagined myself being
anywhere but here.

then He carried me to the peaks
where i saw my way through
and my heart was weightless and
undaunted as that of a child.

i saw the richest of color
where there was none before
and my spirit began to twirl and
leap in the rays of forwardness.

> *You are my hiding place; you will protect me from trouble*
> *and surround me with songs of deliverance.*
> —Psalms 32:7

ON UNFAITHFULNESS

Natural Perspective

The secret is more real
than what is spoken.
The imagined is fueled
by all that's broken.

For the moment there's a fix
for a growing void.
For an hour there's an answer
to the what ifs explored.

For a season there's a *you*
the world's never seen before.
And a soul somewhere
"deserving of what's in store."

Spiritual Perspective

the argument, the betrayal,
the low blows and retreat,
the car, the disappointment—
he's going to let you leave

the keys, the engine
the seed meets the soil
suddenly you remember a face
from seasons passed before

a face that carries memories
of tenderness and truth
of shelter and laughter
that once comforted you

Now your choice lies between
mere thought and indulgence
innocence and justification
the climb and the ledge

Between instinct and impulse
the sniff and the bite
coincidence and the created
God's voice and the lies

No pain is catalyst enough
worth the witness of His name
No closet is dark enough
His presence can't be escaped—

Listen.

There is nothing concealed that will not be disclosed, or hidden that will not be made known. What you have said in the dark will be heard in the daylight, and what you have whispered in the ear in the inner rooms will be proclaimed from the roofs.

—Luke 12:2–3

ON SELF-LOVE

Natural Perspective

To love him was to
forego my own name and priorities
and become whole
as if I were created as *half*
half from birth until salvation
half from crown to soles

To love him was to
finally be among the blessed
—among the aristocracy
marginally qualified, counted fortunate
summoned from the fields
where like-textures and tone should be

To love him was to
sit ignorant of their vices
choosing peace above dignity
deaf to their insults
blind to their evil
numb to their cruelty

Spiritual Perspective

Love doesn't feel at all
the way I envisioned it would

It stripped me of my trinkets
and aged me in wisdom

It washed away my war paint
and the pheromones that attracted him

It cleaned my looking glass
and I see me more beautifully than ever

It removed the calluses on my feet
and gave me glass slippers

It opened my cell—and I love myself
for mustering the courage to walk through

Because a year ago, had that key been turned
I would have traded my freedom for weekend visits

> *Love is patient, love is kind. It does not envy, it does not boast,*
> *it is not proud. It does not dishonor others, it is not self-seeking,*
> *it is not easily angered, it keeps no record of wrongs. Love*
> *does not delight in evil but rejoices with the truth. It always*
> *protects, always trusts, always hopes, always perseveres.*
> —1 Corinthians 13:4–7

ON STARTING AGAIN
(RELATIONSHIPS)

Natural Perspective

He wooed and beckoned her as he often does
With words like Iris and Lily in bloom
Staged so rooms look to inhabit love
Though short-lived are their petals and hues

She closed her eyes and listened to his words
Dried her cheeks and tried to imagine
Seasonal sentiments withered in vases
Replaced by a thriving garden

Where kindness is no seldom deed staged
But is seeded bountifully in the earth
And awakened faithfully after winter's rest
By the breath of He who loves past words

She wandered the beautifully appointed rooms
Then kissed her beau goodbye
"I've seen the garden that awaits and
It needs no middleman to thrive."

Spiritual Perspective

I didn't have to
show Him just
where it hurt
I didn't bother
to fill in any
blanks

His whispers
to my heart
were a balm
confirming He was
with me when I came
this way

My head was
heavy and in search
of rest
I fell limp in the
haven of a custom
embrace

I didn't realize
the hour tears
stopped flowing
or when the scab
formed and peeled
away

Behold, I am doing a new thing; now it
springs forth, do you not perceive it?
—Isaiah 43:19

Shout for joy, you heavens; rejoice, you earth; burst into
song, you mountains! For the Lord comforts his people
and will have compassion on his afflicted ones.
—Isaiah 49:13

ON LOSS OF FAITH

It is with lead that I paint and render to you hues of the mind, body, and soul. What will come of it? There may be strokes of crimson, and there may be strokes of ash; but at this point, they are few and without form, hollow and enveloped by blankness, or they are not there at all.

I don't recall the day or hour, the sky or season, the said or the unsaid. What I know is that your canvas is as incomplete as mine was.

I cannot depict for you a hero. I cannot portray a warrior who would seek justice to ensure that there would be no other prey. Nor can I describe a child who would knowingly betray her due allegiance and muster enough love to rescue herself.

At this point, I cannot paint for you schoolyards, neighboring hoods, or hang outs. They were not pertinent or real for me anymore. There was no innocence left. There was nothing for me there.

Faces that I had actively sought wounds ago were nameless to me now. Pastimes that once filled me with delight and carelessness were humdrum and insufficient. Accomplishments that were incomparable in my yesterdays were amateur and lacked true challenge. Characters that once staked my attention and imagination became shallow and silly overnight. Reruns and sitcoms that could immobilize me before were now noted for their omission of love and romance and were, therefore, abandoned like the church pews during most football seasons.

To sketch a steeple in reflection of this winter in my journey would even be hypocritical. I found myself at square one spiritually, as if I had no foundation at all. Almost every other day, I asked myself, "How is it that one—who was once so consistently engulfed in God's service, worship, and Word—could gradually be wrung like a dishrag and hung to dry."

The dynamics of my spirituality had fizzled to be equal to those of a pancake being flipped, a faucet turning hot then cold, or a summer fling as the—ember months draw nigh. So here I was constrained by my own conditioning. Crippled by imbalances of the tenets of religion and the practice of faith. I was unwilling to receive help because of my own shame, thus perpetually deceived. My version? God had abandoned me in the moment that I needed Him most. Period.

I became a faithless, intriguing, A-bra cup captured and caged in a woman's world, attempting to find someone like me. To my misfortune, I did not have to look long or far.

I can illustrate for you—with vivid and brutal truth—the detriment of the wounded and the decaying in companionship. It is a sealed fate—sealed as if to reach to the very back of the cupboards in search of the opaque skull and crossbones corked vial. It is a bond as morbid as that which is shared between two maggot-ridden strangers beneath the dust of neighboring cemetery lots. Regardless, the child in me pushed beyond all else—as only she could.

She—the aching one, the selfless one, the victimized—shoved past the alters, the red lights. She resurfaced in a time and place where it would be nearly impossible for her to survive.

Though wicked moons had pried her flesh from her innocence, her essence returned and clung steadfast. Her exploits became her identity. Her doom was that every piece of her had adjusted—except the most vulnerable—her mind and emotion. She had become so misguided and naive, so angry and disheartened, and so hardened and curious that her exterior persona attracted the beast in men. There was a fragrance of delusion, desperation, and desertion that exuded her and possessed the wild, the lawless, the rebellious. They emerged from their caves. Their keen senses led them. They knew the scent of her flesh, and they knew her scars. She became their own. This time—voluntarily.

See her canvas strokes. Hear her pages, her journey, and all that is not written here.

Reflection

1. How would you categorize your faith walk today? There have been seasons when I would categorize mine as the faucet that drips overnight during freeze warnings as opposed to the one that runs with power. What about you?

2. If you are at a slow drip this week, this month, this year, remember change is an inside job first. Each of the poems written from a spiritual perspective are a testament to the inner work (mind, heart, spirit) that had to progressive take place for me to first see my situation differently (even before it actually changed). The first step was seeing *me* differently, seeing *me* as a righteous extension of Him, in spite of the situation!

ON ALL THINGS ME

Natural Perspective

I, too, embarked on the hailed but
conveniently untimely quest for self

employing trial and error, challenging inhibitions
with no regard for what others felt

gratification was my compass, its needle
quickly adjusted to each whelm of desperation

plowing ahead in the name of goodwill and courage
toward an uncharted destination

I, too, embarked on that journey
tracking prints and scents thought to be mine

Only to creep up to some shadow of a soul
a form devoid, yet righteously guised

I chased this shadow through alleys, underpasses,
and into throngs of fellow self-seekers

Gawking as they rolled about bathing in waste—
the true nectar of that which merely pleases

Oh, I, too, was entitled to a decade—
a year—a slice of discovery

It was of our culture, a mast of progression,
the natural means to destiny

Now I wish the search had opened and shut
with some savory anthology of sonnets or prose

Or in meditation amidst such frolic:
the breath of Spring through the orange cosmos

How I wish I had paused to bandage
the flesh of those wounded in my wake

Or at best, acknowledged such disproportionate reverences:
like that of minimal output and maximum intake

To but think of the den where the specter slept
to reckon with its incapacities

To witness its worship of self-fulfillment
and the altar, upon which it laid eternity

For some, the quest terminates abruptly
when some unforeseen fate lays claim

For me, a renewed discovery ensued
when my quest subjected to a Nobler Name

Spiritual Perspective

This past Winter
was called *Joy*
and You—
its bestselling Author
with noted prior works
Healing and *Love*
incomparable then
but eventually shelved

This past harvest
was called *Heartache*
and You—
now a Stranger passing through
looking for work
in an unwelcoming town
and I was among them
who shooed You away

This past slumber
was called *Rebirth*
and Yours were
the only breasts of sustenance
swollen and dripping of
Grace and *Restoration* and
You yet beckoned me to drink
Lord, help me not forget!

> *But seek ye first the kingdom of God, and his righteousness;*
> *and all these things shall be added unto you.*
> —Matthew 6:33

ON FAITH

Natural Perspective

On the contrary, the morn brought woe
persistent as the eve before

I expected a voice or a knock
rain of heaven or hymn of comfort

a burning bush or glimpse of chariots
a sign—a difference

or perhaps a radiant package
left at my doorstep, marked Joy

Spiritual Perspective

The soul progressively emptied
Fervent prayer had been reduced
To a moment's plea as the palms burn
And the last frayed inch slips through

It was in the ache of wanting
Mind and heart were consumed
The rope was secured to what was held dear
Not to He who could hold you

Now scripture is likened to the spells
Of magicians with twirling wands and dust
For the soul seeks the miracle
That faith has promised us

Frustration manifests anger
Anger is artillery directed
Towards the passivity of the Savior
To provoke the response expected—

An instant disentanglement
Of what took years to create
A one-man rapture, escaping
That for which the compromise was made

Truth was twisted beyond recognition
Somewhere between self and the yearning—
The promise of Faith is not Magic
The promise was always Mercy

Therefore, I urge you brothers, in view of God's mercy,
to offer your bodies as living sacrifices, holy and pleasing
to God—this is your spiritual act of worship.
—Romans 12:1

ON CHURCH HURT

Natural Perspective

Righteous comes like noonday showers
that temper coastal rays
then out *it* goes amidst the wolves
out—just the way *it* came

and we rejoice for hope abounds
when *Righteous* meets Devour
that Holy tongue, gifts, and Ghost
spring mighty in that hour

and that wayward subjects of Dark Night
kneel at the Truth of Day
convicted by Love and the witness
of Him who is The Way

so out *it* goes amidst the wolves
with Holy shout and dance
to shine with peace and gentleness
heal like the Son of Man

and we rejoice for Love abounds
raising our sword and shield
yet the cries of glory hide
moans of *its* yester-kills

and in that fateful hour
when *Righteous* springs with might
the arrogance of Dark Night
is met with *Righteous Pride*

dark lies of the Devour
meet the *illusion of Light*
casting spectrums of twisted perspective
for *the Righteous must be Right*

as the battle wages on
the swing of Godless ways
meets that of *legalism*
Righteous judgment and *disdain*

tongues once dulled by innocence
and *fluent in heavenly language*
are now toothed blades in the carotids—
of devils wheezing in anguish

soon nowhere in the clanging of swords
or the howling of the night
is Holy tongue, gift, or Ghost
is *Righteous shout or cry*

but all are howling and dripping crimson
with exposed claw and fang
all are howling then away they go
away—just the way they came

somewhere along the journey back
beneath the cover of night
Righteous reclaims its sword and shield
again becomes a *sheepish sight*

and then springs forth as we rejoice
lifting up shout and shield
and go on training—searching pews
for the next *Righteous kill*

Spiritual Perspective

I paid a visit to My house
one arbitrary Tuesday;
loved that you named it Upon This Rock
such an inspired name.

Noticed the lions carved in stone
guarding the arched doorways.
Vast is the stretch across aisle and nave,
no short abundance of space.

Noticed the chancel was adorned
with banners proclaiming My Words.
And above hung flags for every tongue,
every nation in the world.

I paid a visit to My house;
stood outside the bustling vestries
and heard the gossip of the week
compliments of the lay leads.

In the trash—a discarded bulletin:
The biannual missions' trip is nigh!
Also, a benevolence application
sent by one I know—Denied?

I took the stairs to The Lounge,
a sanctuary for the youth,
on the walls were portraits
the pride of your "Who's Who?"

I paid a visit to My house;
pristine was the café.
Among aromas of Nestle and mocha
was the fragrance of dismay.

Two volunteers sunken in despair
cried and commiserated,
sharing flesh lashes from the whip
of cliques owned by the rich and educated

Displayed in the bookstore were
covers bearing familiar names—
names feared as holding both the whip and keys
to the cliques that run this place

I paid a visit to My house;
blinding lights and columns high.
I paid a visit to My house;
problem is, it was not Mine!

By this everyone will know that you are my
disciples, if you love one another.
—John 13:35

If anyone will not welcome you or listen to your words, leave
that home or town and shake the dust off your feet.
—Matthew 10:14

ON SURVIVING

Natural Perspective

Should the truth be captured
your canvas must bleed
It must drip abundantly
of your deepest crimson

You must see, think, and encounter
what you fear most
You must close yourself
to hope, to reason, to home

And open to nakedness,
to helplessness, and ruins,
to learned sexuality
and to despair.

Now for the remainder of your vulnerability
wander in that very condition
among priests and beasts, the untaken and the bitten
the fulfilled and the desperate—

With which would you find likeness?

Spiritual Perspective

If my blackest nights
were to each be painted a face,
given a ghastly stature,
and called by a name

There would be a militia
a legion charging my gates
and should I stand alone
I'd need only speak One Name

The Name that commands angel armies,
shuts the mouth of the king of beasts
with horses and chariots of fire,
brings legions to their knees

> Some trust in chariots and some in horses, but we
> trust in the name of the Lord our God.
>
> —Psalms 20:7

ON PRAYER

A Call to Action

I had resolved to end the eve praying
and so the night began as they all do;
my *Intent* and *Nature* standing squarely
gun slingin' like the westerns on the tube.

And so the tumble weed began to roll.
Townsmen tucked to peek from 'round the bend.
Intent paced-off from Web, email and phone.
Nature paced from all likes of discipline.

Half-starved hounds carried off their porch scraps.
Salon doors creaked back and forth until still.
Angry gusts swept over the wagon tracks.
Dust funnels swirled and then disappeared.

And there upon the worn iPad case,
drooled the one who resolved to seek His face.

> *I do not understand what I do. For what I want
> to do I do not do, but what I hate I do.*
>
> —Romans 7:15

> *Then he returned to his disciples and found them sleeping. "Simon,"
> he said to Peter, "are you asleep? Couldn't you keep watch for one
> hour? Watch and pray so that you will not fall into temptation.
> The spirit is willing, but the flesh is weak.*
>
> —Mark 14: 37–38

ON CHRISTIANITY

A Call to Action

The Golden Arches called to me
as they did in my youth.
I had no choice but to answer
my tummy's grumbles for instant crude.

I leapt from car to threshold
to see if it all had changed:
the golden fries, shiny buns,
sundaes and fruit parfaits.

I expected a tiled pathway
that's swept and mopped though worn,
leading to bleached white counters
like mom's kitchen had back home.

And there would stand some smiling soul
like in the advertisements,
some soul beaming with pride
based on belief in the arches.

Just like a florist who foresees
the joy of his bouquet,
upon finding the hands and heart
for whom the gift was made.

Or like the righteous who discerns
the voids of those in the alter line,
serving up Truth and Love,
certain the product satisfies.

But, when I swung open the door
and glanced down at my path…
dried ketchup splattered mosaics
smashed fries and bits of trash

Choosing my steps, I made my way
up to the counter where
two employees stepped in the ring
no cameras, bell or ref'.

The "smiling souls" began to swear
and turned stark raging mad.
There was much more back there cooking than
Happy Meals and Big Macs.

The two went to their corners when
the manager approached;
One finally took my order
with an air of reproach.

I got the order I came for
and sat it on my car dash.
The visit made me second guess
the contents of the bag.

I never took one single bite,
just simply drove away
trying to recall what it was
that made the arches great?

Like the range of emotions from
the heart that's been devout
upon finding unfaithfulness
from an uncaring spouse.

Or like the Savior who observes
the masses that profess
to live according to His name…
by spirit, not by flesh.

The masses that live by and teach
versions of the Bible
that shift to fit the cravings of
culture and flesh, not the soul.

The masses that will flash His name
like one would flash a badge,
but are about a life purpose
unlike the one He had.

For in our struggle to compete,
appease or reinvent,
we've ensured each encounter feels
like false advertisement.

By their fruit you will recognize them…
—Matthew 7:16

Not everyone who says to me, 'Lord, Lord,' will enter
the kingdom of heaven, but only the one who does
the will of my Father who is in heaven.
—Matthew 7:21

ABOUT THE AUTHOR

Gomer is a survivor of long-standing domestic violence and sexual, emotional, and spiritual abuse. With these overlapping experiences spanning her most impressionable years, the resulting struggle was (and is) to redefine boundaries, faith, and self-image. She tried everything—"Godly counsel," trial and error, painkillers, isolation, active church attendance. She was stuck! The game changer was realizing deliverance is an inside job that is utterly dependent on a relentless pursuit of God and righteous commitment to self. Every move with respect to that inside job of deliverance is a move in *Love* (this world's most misrepresented work of all). Gomer's life and words speak to that inside job—our inside job!